Manufactured by Amazon.ca
Acheson, AB

15492899R00068